COWBOY JUNKIES

XX

WITH WATERCOLORS BY
ENRIQUE MARTINEZ CELAYA

WHALE AND STAR

CONTENTS

A HORSE IN THE COUNTRY

                    A   E
The money would be pretty good if a quart of milk was still a dollar
      Bb   A
or even if a quart of milk was still a quart
         D   A
And the hours I dont mind the way the creeps on by like the old love I use
       Bb   E   A
its the jives that syph dangers that are doing me in
          D   ...D. that ok

      D   Dm   A
cos I've got a horse out _ the country
  Bb   E   D-eity D A
I got to see him every send sunday
 Fdm   Bb   Dm   A
he aint who I call him, yet he has his name
     Bb   E
one day ~~~~~~~~~~ will saddle ~
         Bb   the two of us will ride away   A A7 E A
                    D   E   A
Guess I would be gay, yeah is ~ yet to young
    Bb   A
but somtimes you need somsone and your guts, yet here
  D   E   A
its not that I don't love him anymore it yet that when I hear
                   D   Bb   E
him come through the front door my heart don't ~~~ like
        A
it did once before

And all my friends have settled down
become their (Db) mothers + their fathers without (A) a sound (E)
except for (E) Cathy, she bought a one way subway ticket (D)
And left us all (A) behind

but that's not for me...

(CHORUS) |

(A)
This town wouldn't be so bad
if (E) a girl could trust her instincts (A)
or even (Bb) if a girl could trust a boy (A)

A HORSE IN THE COUNTRY

9

I guess I married too young
Yeah 19 is just too young
But sometime you meet someone.
and your guts just burn
it's not that I don't know how to argue
but when I lay he arm tonight that feel down
my heart doesn't move like it once did before.

but I still wear his ring
and every morning I crawl into bed next to him
when I wake up he's gone

& but I don't mind.

the money would like be so bad pretty good
or a quart of milk was still a dollar
or even if a quart of milk was still a quart
And the hours I don't mind
the way they easily and carelessly pass on by like an old friend of mine
its those years that just seem to disappear
that are doing me in

and each night at closing time
It feels like there always 2 me sheets
trying to pull in me a line
and the sheets open a little darker
just keep going a little now old night by night

but I don't mind

SUN

Gd't

cheap.

zoo

Devil

marvan

~~singwalig~~ gwalig

Jane

House

~~oak~~ Bury

walking

———————

Tonight ~~catif~~ Blue ~~walking~~

Sling

Kidd

Jane.

Escape.

Son

Witches

Lonesome

~~Bury~~ Angel

DUST

Kidd ~

Escape ~

Jane ~

Sling ~

Sun.

Bea's Song   part 2 of "River Song Trilogy"

(C) ~~January~~   At my feet
The Speed river running low and flat
I'm (Am) sitting here burning daylight thinking about the past (C)
And (F) that distance out there where the earth reach the sky,
(F) The slightest move and this river mud pulls me (F) further down
(G) John's at my side, but he's (E) sitting on firmer ground.

John says I look at the moon and the stars (more often)(these days)
than I look into his eyes
And I can't disagree so I don't say nothing
I just stare on past his face at Venus rising
like a shining disc of hope hanging over the horizon

With each passing year that I sit here
that horizon seems to yield just that much nearer
And all that ~~piles up~~ appears and seems is as clear as spit
but if there's one thing in my life that the years have taught it's
that you can always see it coming but you can never stop it.

                At my feet
The Speed river running low and flat
I'm sitting here burning daylight thinking about the past
and that distance out there where the earth meets the sky
x2 { The slightest move and this river mud pulls me further down
    { John's at my side, but he's not noticing that I'm drowning.

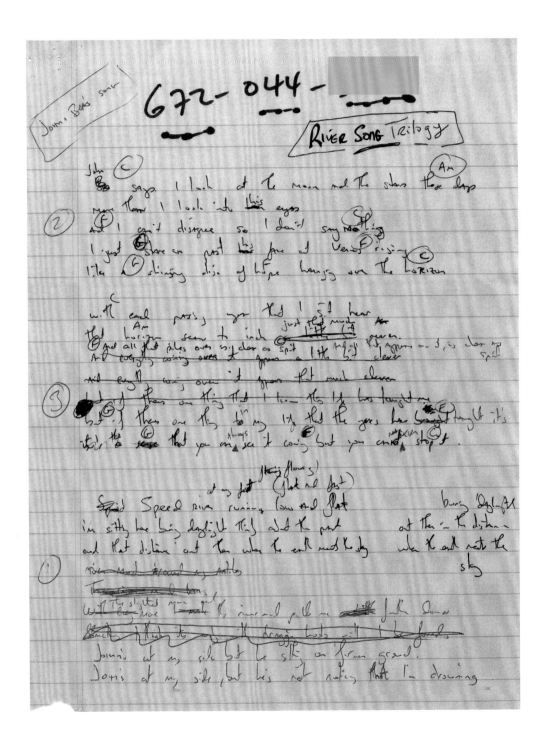

Now I know, ~~what it fee~~ Now I know what ~~it's like~~ it's means to Broken

Now I know, know I know what is ~~like~~ means to be bared

You in the chair ~~uneasily~~, ~~red worthless~~ absently/systematically sinking ~~s~~

Now I know, Now I know what its like to be ~~saved~~.

I'm on my knees, ~~without~~ ~~Afraid OF THE world~~ once agri made aware ~~out there~~ ~~a word or comfort to~~ spare.

~~there's life out there~~

~~MADE AWARE~~

Grief is a ~~feeling~~ word ~~that~~ to describes the absence of feeling

Now I know, Now I know, know I mean ~~now nothing~~ what ~~is like~~ it means to be ~~Remembered~~

and out your load to the
crescent moon
Grass Hold by the hollow

Swallow

The Ked moon is waning

Like the moon my love's waning

HOWARD JOHNSON LODGES & HOTELS
Cambridge (617) 492-7777 • Revere (617) 284-7200 • Maine (207) 873-3335
Boston (Kenmore) (617) 267-3100 • Boston (Fenway) (617) 267-8300

She placed her ring on the sill
~~dishes~~ dishes piled high
she's on the front porch step
And the air smells like snow
~~and she~~, ~~thinking~~ of the siege ~~to come~~
~~where every living thing~~ ~~must fight to stay alive~~
And how she'll miss those weekends in
the porch with the sun ~~on her face~~
~~in her face~~ and her book by her side
And that lingering taste
That he left on her tongue

He ~~placed~~ his glass from the ~~table~~ hall
it leaves a ring where it stood.
He ~~peers~~ ~~through~~ the window he looks at the window he sees the light from the window
~~and~~ ~~her sitting~~ ~~below~~ ~~at the light~~ below ~~(as the light washes)~~ body caressing her out there
And he's remembering the first time he kissed her caressing her out there
And how he'd wake and immediately miss her
Like a smell with her taste
her breath ~~irritating~~ as hell

{ C   G   F   C
  C   G   Dm   Dm/maj7 C }   insistent Break

He puts her ring on her finger
brushes back her hair

everything they value under siege
~~Bridge?~~ { thought that not days but
but nothing that you can hold
on to
staying with the ___ in her for

{ each breath he tastes her
breath like a harsh
irritating as hell

not days but passed on through
cause there was nothing there
for her to hold on to

RING ON THE SILL

Have you ever seen a sight a beautiful
as that of the rain soaked purple.
of the white birch in Spring

                    more   on
have you ever felt as fresh ~~or as wonderful~~
~~Rhythm~~
~~in~~ or a warm fall night under a mackerel sky,
the smell of grapes on the wind

Well I have known all these things
and the joys that they can bring
~~but~~ I'll ~~trade~~ them for a cup of coffee
And to wear your ring

have you ever had the pleasure of watching
a quiet winters snow slowly gathering
like simple moments adding up   🏠 3.3.18

have you ever satisfied a gut feeling
to follow a dry dirt road ~~thats~~ beckoning
you to the heart of a shimmering summer day

Well I have known all these things
and the joys that they can bring
~~but~~ I'll ~~trade~~ them all for a cup of coffee
And to wear your ring

Escape Is So

Simple

F
The ___ you kissed me
this morning
it told me
that you soon would
be B♭ goin

Gm   C7
you didn't even look in my eyes
when you said goodbye F

see ____ ___ ___ ____
~~___ ___ ___ ___~~
and last night
in your sleep
~~you ___ ___ ___~~
you broke all the _____
that I knew you could never keep

Gm
now I'm ready to leave
while you ___ in the _____
Bb
and you a ___ ___ ___ down the road F
Bb 5

Bb
___ is so simple
in ___ would ____ sunsets on be ____ F
but distance only ____ the ___ Bb
___ ___ of F: so we always be myself
Bb   Dm   Am ___ ___ C/F

~~There we said~~
Yeah I remember
how we said ____.
was the craziest word
that we knew.

but I ___ ___ I like to meet better
than to ~~do so long~~ goodbye

♩ ♩♩♩ ♩
♩♩   All I could sit here ____
at the ___ all ___
and ___ of the _____
only you are not by my side

instead I'll go to the kitchen
find a strong drink to sit in
and drink myself further away

a verse in "crescent moon"
About looking at person but not
seeing the real person — maybe reach
a hand to that person.

❄ Holiday Inn
GATEWAY CENTER

US 30, & Iowa State Center Exit Post Office Box X, Ames, Iowa 50010 515-292-8600

34

YOU WILL BE LOVED AGAIN

(Mary Margaret O'Hara)

How could he take you in his arms
and help you to be free
then leave you forgotten
and is it enough to cry?
When you're so broken...

Her cold eyes tell you you're not welcome
she tells lies but you'll take her back again
and is it enough to die?
When you're so taken.

You will be loved again
You will be loved again

But will he sing
and will he dance
and will he forever
and will she sing
and will she dance
and will she forever

Someday you will feel a love so deep
and you'll find someone not lost in sleep

And you will be loved again
you will be loved again
you will be loved again

And they're thinking of the long road ahead
And the strength that they will need just to reach the end
And there in the silence they wait for the night
to embrace the few that they feel with the love that they know is right
And there in the silence they search for the balm
to drown the fear that haunts them and a love that has passed them by

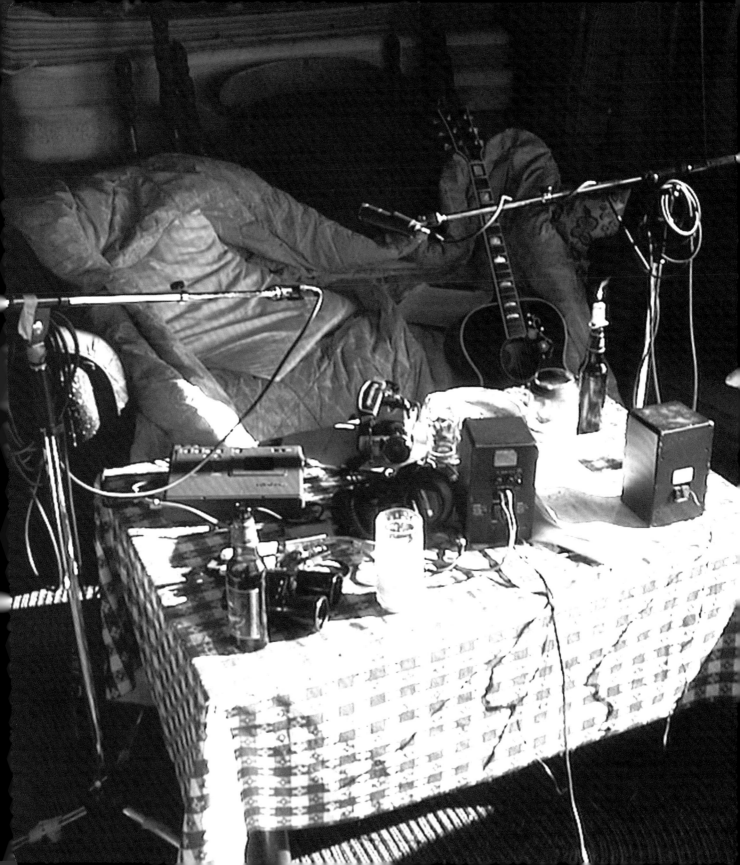

he could be as distant as the walls of Arthur's castle
or he could be as warm as the first day of spring

and All I loved him, didn't I?

Baptists joyfully with praise to the Lord
Shedrunkg ??? ???
fire & forth ??? celebrity yet sing
each other again
but tomorrow I'll be gone again

murder in the trailer park tonight.
It is Fiona percy found with her neck slashed. It's a Life
homicide dick tying yellow ribbons round her site. A veteran
red chemise slashing up the night, Fiona ....
identifies the body, lets out a bloom chillingscream.
.... been a murder in the trailer park tonight

~~A murder dies her most~~
Murder in the trailer park tonight
Another body I've got 160 dollars in my pocket and
I felt that I gave in the Ford
if we leave now we can read .... before dawn .... !
I tell ~~park get this money wet ... out it ... out the~~
watching things at the ~~trash transit~~
Make your things then there I want to wash the dirt
before daylight ~~tumble tumble~~
I ...... it counting mid night watching things at the truckmount
with I ain't got none you on my car care do you
bitchin too ... if the colours right that should be good enough
are you coming or are you abandoning me too

Murder ... dies in trailer park tonight

Its the kind of night thats so cold; when you spit
it freezes before it hits the ground
And when a bum asks you for a quarter you guarantees dollar,
if he's out tonight, he must be truly down
And I'm searching all the windows for a last minute present
to prove to you the words I spoke were real
something small and frail and plastic, baby
cause cheap is how I feel.

Half moon in the sky tonight, bright enough
to come up with an answer
to the question why is it that every time I see you
my love grows a little bigger
But your ~~recent~~

~~like a lie your about to be revealed~~
~~but of a few weeks~~
cause cheap is how I feel

3/15
7
14/5

	600	700
	65	
	775	

(your body for a, soul)

Its not the small is hear that gets very but the lighting
I hate the shadows that it casts
And the sound of clink bottles is the one suits
that I'll always drag it one for my past
I think I'll find a ~~pair~~ of guys tonight to talk to
And maybe strike a deal
My body for your soul, fair swap
cause cheap is how I feel.

adam's mark.
charlotte

the dark.

e down / A
         much
         mystery.

the always meant to say the song
for those words I left unsaid
~~Sorry~~ "Sorry", I feel better ~~now~~, do you?
and if we meet again as strangers
let's ~~keep it that way this time~~ let it stay that way
give it a rest for another ~~life~~ generation or two.

B   Em   Am
you'll never find the path I'm leaving
     even though you know the path I walk
Am) C   (c) Am   Em   Am
   footsteps leaving no footprints in the sand
     But when   Em the time comes for you C to follow
     just Am look to the right E sky
I'll Am be the one C reaching out my ~~hand~~ G

G   Em
Black eyed man beneath the earth /   with the rope burn round your neck
twing winter into spring   do you still enjoy the pleasure you bring

Black eyed man I'll always keep him close in mind

Please tell us what'd he say
~~before~~ in his cell the night before

F   C   G

And I don't know how I survived those days
before I held your hand
       G   C
yes always thought of myself as a lonely man
there as much more ~~know~~ to think about
and (F) (C) to understand   ~~# #~~ (F) (bb?)
how ~~with~~ the touch of your hand
    G
you ~~can see the only thought I'm thinking~~

And I don't know how I survived those days
before I held your hand
~~always thought of myself C A lonely man~~

54

Thousand
~~year~~ prayer

Here we ~~are~~ all are at the end of "the century of beauty lost"
We greedily ate what you gave us, the rest we tossed.
We've trapped all your rivers, paved every pass
pulled at your sky till we caused it to rip.
P.   But you've got Jimi Hendrix, so let's call it an even split.

I've met a girl who ~~has~~ has turned my whole world upside down
The stars I once stretched for now litter the ground.
I ~~am~~ cursed by too little   or ~~was~~ is it too much, belief
(in your ~~power to deliver defeat~~)   in the strength of another mans words
                                            (power)
But I've got a girl, thank you lord

Here we all are at the start of another thousand ~~years~~.
All those love stories, yet to be told.
~~Our love is a blessing in the form~~
Our ~~love~~ is this river, ~~what flows at our feet.~~   asleep ~~start~~ at our feet and
~~kssel by~~ ~~tossed~~ ~~big~~ this wet autumn day.
Here we all are ~~start at the start of further day~~.
~~at tomorrow while to say~~

murder ... in the trail pool tight

Miss Fiona Paine found with her neck slashed after dead.

On her dance tryg yellow ribbons round her site again

red dress shots up the night, cutting ... scene

Miss Fion reylen Mary lifts ... the life, cries stood shut,

lets out a lonesome holler hold y scream.

C	Bb	G	Eb
I	vVIIb	v	IIIb
A	G	E	C
E	#D	B	G

F#m	Em	C#m	Am
	Cm/Cm	Cm	
I	vII	v	III

E	F#m	B	D#m	G#m	Bm	Ebm	E
I	IIm	V	VIIm	IVm	Vm	Ibm	I
C	Dm	G	Bm	Em	Gm	Bm/Em	C

something more besides, you

One foot slips before the end

A question formed upon still lips
but I'm afraid to ask it   (but I'll not be the first to ask it) while none will be asked

I guess I believe that there's a point to what we do.

something more besides you
I tell myself one there be something more besides you

A question formed upon still lips
is passed on but never asked

its nearly I spend —
I awake this morning with the bed
small blessings laid before us / little mysteries slowly unfold.

yet still I wonder is there a point to what we do
I kind of doubt that there's something more besides you
although it's hard to find the point in what we do
do I dare to believe that there is something more besides, you.

but I've seen a cloud of starlings rising
~~was hold~~ on a crisp Autumn day.
~~been~~ ~~born felt~~ the weight of a child sleeping
~~Across my chest and on her tummy~~
tasted the tears that fall when saying
good bye forever.
~~speak the words of a life passes~~
I ~~recognize the~~
~~And I'm taught that you always~~
I've seen the silver from a waning moon
wash ~~sky~~ upon a shore

SELECTED LYRICS

200 MORE MILES

Atlanta's a distant memory.
Montgomery a recent blur.
Tulsa burns on the desert floor
like a signal fire.

I got Willie on the radio
a dozen things on my mind
and number one is fleshing out
these dreams of mine.

I've got 200 more miles of rain, asphalt and light
before I sleep.
But there'll be no warm sheets or welcoming arms
to fall into tonight.

In Nashville there is a lighter
in a case for all to see,
it speaks of dreams and heartaches
left unsung.

And in the corner stands a guitar and
lonesome words scrawled in a drunken hand.
I'm travelling paths travelled hard before
and I'm beginning to understand
that I've got 200 more miles of rain, asphalt and light
before I sleep.
But there'll be no warm sheets or welcoming arms
to fall into tonight.

They say that I am crazy,
my life wasting on this road,
that time will find my dreams
scattered dead and cold.

But ahead there is a light
drawing me to reach an end
and when I reach there, I'll turn back,
and you and I can begin again.

I've got 200 more miles of rain, asphalt and light
before I sleep.
But there'll be no warm sheets or welcoming arms
to fall into tonight.

I've got 200 more miles of rain, asphalt and light
before I sleep.
But I wouldn't trade all your golden tomorrows
for one hour of this night.

Atlanta's a distant memory.
Montgomery a recent blur.
Tulsa burns on the desert floor
like a signal fire.

SUN COMES UP, IT'S TUESDAY MORNING

Sun comes up, it's Tuesday morning,
hits me straight in the eye.
Guess you forgot to close the blind last night.
Oh, that's right, I forgot, it was me.

I sure do miss; the smell of black coffee in the morning;
the sound of water splashing all over the bathroom;
the kiss that you would give me even though I was sleeping;
but I kind of like the feel of this extra few feet in my bed.

Telephone's ringing, but I don't answer it
cause everybody knows that good news always sleeps till noon.
Guess it's tea and toast for breakfast again,
maybe I'll add a little T.V. too.

No milk! God, how I hate that.
Guess I'll go to the corner, get breakfast from Jenny.
She's got a black eye this morning, "Jen how'd ya get it?"
She says, "Last night, Bobby got a little bit out of hand."

Lunchtime. I start to dial your number,
then I remember so I reach for something to smoke.
And anyways I'd rather listen to Coltrane
than go through all that shit again.

There's something about an afternoon spent doing nothing;
just listening to records and watching the sun falling;
thinking of things that don't have to add up to something;
and this spell won't be broken
by the sound of keys scraping in the lock.

Maybe tonight it's a movie,
with plenty of room for elbows and knees
a bag of popcorn all to myself.
Black and white, with a strong female lead
and if I don't like it, no debate, I'll leave.

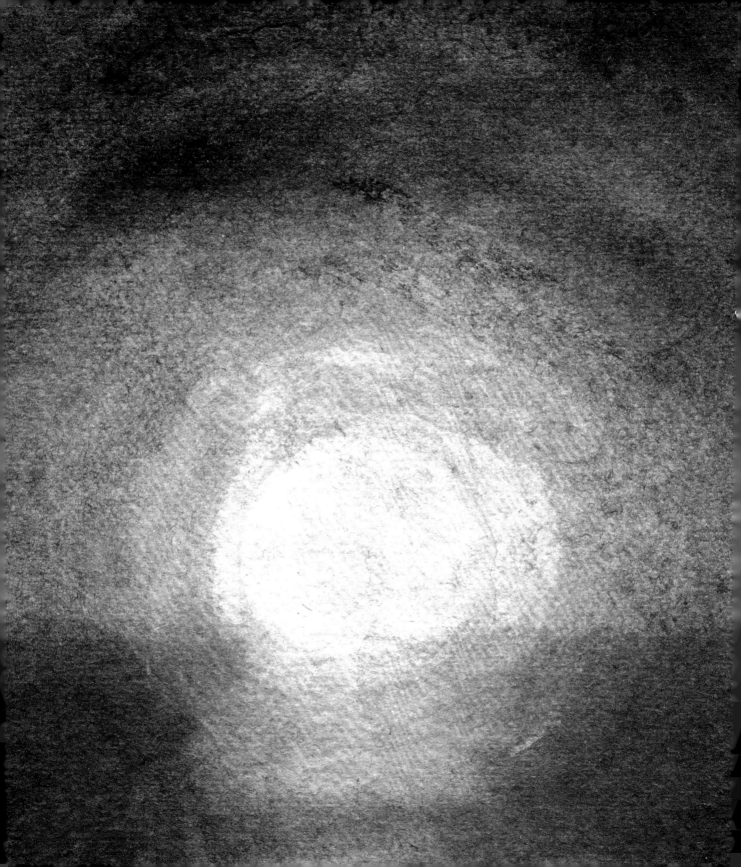

Here comes that feeling that I'd forgotten:
how strange these streets feel at night
when you're alone on them.
Each pair of eyes just filled with suggestion.
So I lower my head, make a beeline for home,
seething inside.

Funny, I'd never noticed
the sound the streetcars make as they pass my window.
Which reminds me that I forgot to close the blind again.

Yeah, sure I'll admit there are times when I miss you.
Especially like now when I need someone to hold me.
But there are some things that can never be forgiven.
And I've just got to tell you
that I kind of like this extra few feet in my bed.

WHERE ARE YOU TONIGHT

There's a young man in the corner playing *Crazy* all night long,
quarters piled high upon the table.
He orders Wild Turkey and with a quick wit and a smile
he says, "My darling, you're the one I'll drape in sable."
But his baseball cap and this bar-room rap
tell me a different story:
this is not the prince to grant my wishes.
Just another lonely country-boy grown weary of the night.
Just another boy with a sink full of dirty dishes.

Where are you tonight?
When I left you in my dreams last night
you promised me that we would be breaking free.
Where are you tonight?

He tells me of the back roads
and how we'll drive them all night long.
How the days will fade and the moon will hang forever.
And how the cloud of dust we'll kick up will linger like a song.
And how the myth will grow about the two who refused to surrender.

Then I catch us in the bar-room mirror
with his arm around my shoulder:
this girl I see has grown so unfamiliar.
And as she stands to leave with a stranger by her side,
she can't help but laugh at a life grown so peculiar.

Where are you tonight?
I don't think I can face tomorrow's light
not knowing if you'll be there to guide me.
Where are you tonight?

Where are you tonight?
I think that I'll make it through all right,
but I'd love to have you, just one more time, beside me.

'CAUSE CHEAP IS HOW I FEEL

It's the kind of night that's so cold when you spit
it freezes before it hits the ground.
And when a bum asks you for a quarter, you give a dollar,
if he's out tonight he must be truly down.
And I'm searching all the windows for a last minute present
to prove to you what I said was real,
for something small and frail and plastic, baby,
'cause cheap is how I feel.

Half moon in the sky tonight, bright enough
to come up with an answer
to the question: why is it that every time I see you
my love grows a little stronger?
But your memory leaves my stomach churning,
feeling like a lie about to be revealed.
But I'll horde all this to myself
'cause cheap is how I feel.

It's not the smell in here that gets to me it's the lights,
I hate the shadows that they cast.
And the sound of clinking bottles is the one thing
I'll always drag with me from my past.
I think I'll find a pair of eyes tonight
to fall into and maybe strike a deal:
your body for my soul, fair swap,
'cause cheap is how I feel.

ROCK AND BIRD

She captured both Rock and Bird,
tied one to the leg of the other.
Kept them as prisoners
until they knew who was master.
Then she threw them to the sky.

Bird with unbarred wings disappeared.
Rock with weighted heart returned.
And Rock became her anchor.
And Bird became her dream.

Now she stands on the forest floor
among the pines and towering firs.
Rock still firm beneath her feet,
Bird perched high above her
singing songs of love's betrayal.

"I offered you my endless skies
you countered with hoods and chains.
This song I sing will be the last
to be inspired by your memory."

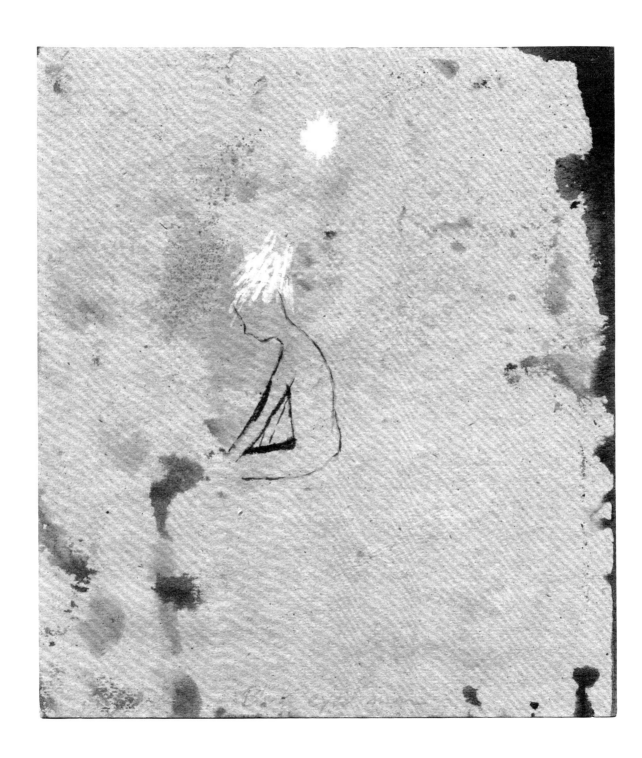

BLACK EYED MAN

Black eyed man, he took the blame
for the poisoning of the well.
They found his shoes by the pulley.
They found his fingerprints all over the pail.

Black eyed man I'm warning you;
the people around here
will not be fooled by a simple line or two.

Yes your honour I do solemnly swear
that I saw him late that night,
dancing barefoot, bathed in light
and reaching for every star in sight.
Yes I did go to him,
but completely against my will
and yes he did things to me,
things of which I dream of still.

Black eyed man I'm warning you;
what I say is what you'll do,
to hell with love and truth.

I always meant to say I'm sorry
for the things I said and did.
Sorry. I feel better now, do you?
But you promised me the sky
and fell short a star or two.
What else did you expect me to do?

Black eyed man, he took the blame
for the poisoning of the well.
They found his shoes by the pulley.
They found his fingerprints all over the pail.
With a noose around his neck,
cicadas trilling everywhere,
he says to the people gathered round him,
"it ain't the water that's not right around here."

Black eyed man, I'm thirsty dear,
be a love and bring some water here
drawn fresh from the well.

A HORSE IN THE COUNTRY

The money would be pretty good if a quart of milk was still a dollar
or even if a quart of milk was still a quart.
And the hours, well, I don't mind how they creep on by like an old friend of mine,
it's the years that simply disappear that are doing me in.

Guess I married too young, yeah nineteen was just too young,
but sometimes you meet someone and your guts just burn.
It's not that I don't love him anymore
it's just that when I hear him coming through that front door
my heart doesn't race like it did once before.

But I've got a horse out in the country.
I get to see him every second Sunday.
He comes when I call him, yeah he knows his name,
one day we'll saddle up and the two of us will ride away.

This weather I could almost stand if the sun would shine a little brighter,
or even if the sun would shine at all.
But lately it just seems to me that this life has lost its mystery
and these cold fall mornings seem to bite just a little bit harder.

And all my friends have settled down,
become their mothers and their fathers without a sound,
except for Cathy; she bought a one way subway ticket and left us all behind.

But I've got a horse out in the country.
I get to see him every second Sunday.
He comes when I call him, yeah he knows his name,
one day I'll saddle up and the two of us will ride away.

This town wouldn't be so bad if a girl could trust her instincts,
or even if a girl could trust a boy.

MURDER, TONIGHT, IN THE TRAILER PARK

Murder tonight in the trailer park.
Mrs. Annabelle Evans found
with her throat cut, after dark.
Her pockets turned inside out
her dresser drawers turned upside down.
Anna's neighbour, Peg, identifies the body,
lets out a hollow kind of sound.

Homicide is tying yellow ribbons
around her silver Airstream.
Red cherries slashing up the night,
cutting through that cordoned crime scene.
There's been a murder in the trailer park tonight.

Murder tonight in the trailer park.
"Pack your things, Ann Marie,
we're heading west,
we're going to make a fresh start.
I've been saving pennies,
been looking forward to this day.
No time for questions,
are you coming, or are you going to stay?"

Crosstown at the Waterton
George Evans is sitting tall and tight,
buying drinks for all the regulars,
bragging about how them bones
danced for him tonight.
There's been a murder in the trailer park tonight.

Murder tonight in the trailer park.
Faceless man counting crumpled bills,
hotel neon fights the dark.
TV set in the corner, they're talking murder
on the late-night news.

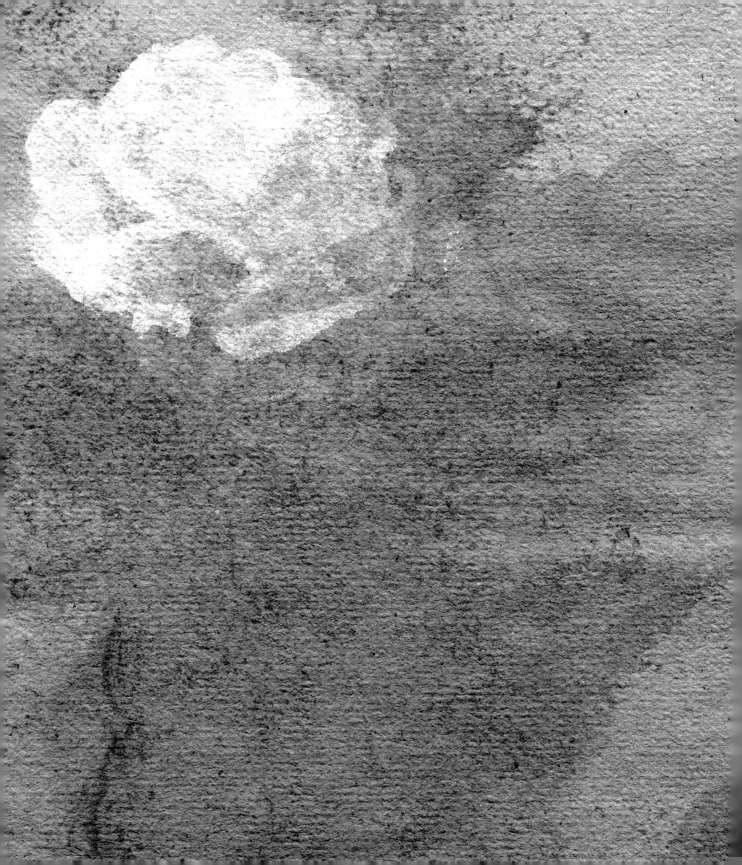

He turns down the sound, waits for the sports,
he only wants to know, "did I win or did I lose?"

There's been a murder in the trailer park tonight.

THIS STREET, THAT MAN, THIS LIFE

This street holds its secrets
like a cobra holds its kill.
This street minds its business
like a jailer minds his jail.
That house there is haunted.
That door's a portal to hell.
This street holds its secrets very well.

That man wears his skin
like a dancer wears her veils.
That man stalks his victim
like a cancer stalks a cell.
That man's soul has left him
his heart's as deadly as a rusty nail.
That man sheds his skin like a veil.

Lord, you play a hard game,
you know we follow every rule.
Then you take the one thing
that we thought we'd never lose.
All I ask, is if she's with you
please keep her warm and safe
and if it's in your power
please purge the memory of this place.

This life holds its secrets
like a seashell holds the sea,
soft and distant, calling
like a fading memory.
This life has its victories,
but its defeats tear so viciously.
This life holds its secrets
like the sea.

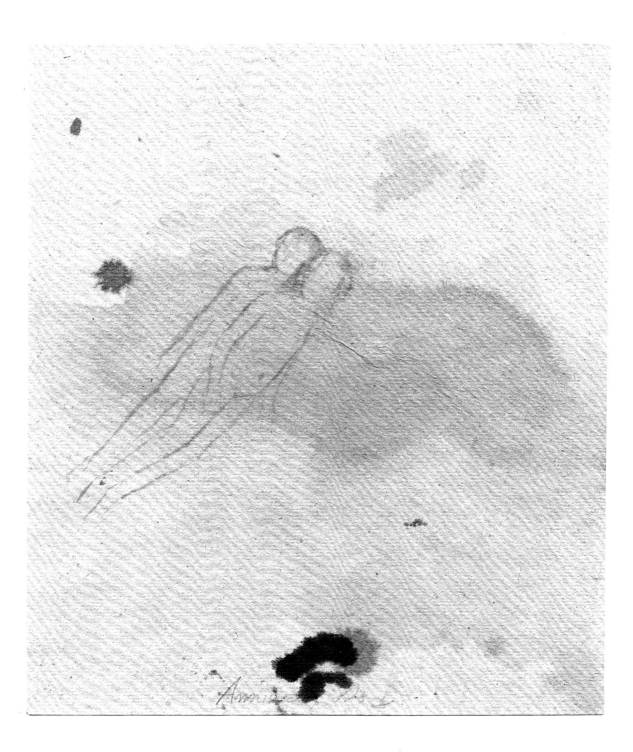

ANNIVERSARY SONG

Have you ever seen a sight as beautiful
as that of the rain-soaked purple
of the white birch in spring?

Have you ever felt more fresh or wonderful
than on a warm fall night
under a mackerel sky,
the smell of grapes on the wind?

Well I have known all these things
and the joys that they can bring.
And I'll share them all for a cup of coffee
and to wear your ring.

Have you ever had the pleasure of watching
a quiet winter's snow slowly gathering
like simple moments adding up?

Have you ever satisfied a gut feeling
to follow a dry dirt road that's beckoning you
to the heart of a shimmering summer's day?

Well I have known all these things
and the joys that they can bring.
And I'll share them all for a cup of coffee
and to wear your ring.

And I don't know how I survived those days
before I held your hand.
Well, I never thought that I would be the one,
to admit that the moon and the sun
shine so much more brighter, when
seen through two pairs of eyes than
when seen through just one.

Have you ever seen a sight as beautiful
as a face in a crowd of people
that lights up just for you?

Have you ever felt more fresh or wonderful
as when you wake
by the side of that boy or girl
who has pledged their love to you?

Well I have known all these things
and the joys that they can bring.
And now every morning there's a cup of coffee
and I wear your ring.

FIRST RECOLLECTION

My first recollection is a day in December;
black iron steam engine covered in ice,
like some Precambrian monster,
moaning and snorting.
Nothing was ever going to beat that beast
in a fair fight.

I've sat and watched the woodpiles
grow through the summer.
Now I'm sitting, smelling summer burn through the fall.
Winter's coming on, days getting dreary
and I'm thinking this is the season
that I leave you all.

I've heard a man in crisis
falls back on what he knows best:
a murderer to murder,
a thief to theft.
And I don't want you to think
that this is some kind of deathbed confession.
But run is what I did when put to the test.

My first recollection is a day in December;
747 tracing lines through the sky,
like some old gypsy curse,
silently preying upon the dreams of those
who jealously watch life pass by.

I've sat and watched my troubles
pile through the summer.
Now I'm sitting, hearing my youngest cry
down the hall.
Winter's coming on, days getting dreary
and I'm thinking this is the season
that I leave you all.

I've heard that the son must bear
the burdens of the father,
but it's the daughter that is left
to clean up the mess.
And I don't want you to think
that I'm asking for absolution.
But run is what I did when put to the test.

RING ON THE SILL

She placed her ring on the sill,
dishes piled high.
She's on the front porch step
and the air smells like snow.
She's thinking of the siege to come
and how she'll miss those weekends
in the park, with the sun on her face
and her book by her side and that
lingering taste that he left on her tongue.

He lifts his glass from the table,
it leaves a ring where it stood.
He sees the light from the window
caress her like he knows he should.
He's remembering the first time he kissed her
and how he'd wake
and immediately he'd miss her;
like a spell, with each breath
he'd taste her breath, like a haunting,
irritating as hell.

Do you remember when you'd pray
to never see the day
when someone would make you feel this way?
'Cause you knew
they would cut right through you
and once inside you were afraid they'd find
nothing to hold on to.

He puts her ring on her finger,
she brushes back his hair.
He takes a sip from his glass,
she inhales the cold fall air.

And they're thinking of the long road ahead
and the strength that they will need
just to reach the end.
And there in the silence, they search
for the balance, between this fear that they feel
and a love that has graced their lives.

BEA'S SONG (RIVER SONG TRILOGY: PART II)

Speed River at my feet running low and flat,
I'm sitting here burning daylight,
thinking about the past
and that distance out there
where the earth meets the sky.
The slightest move and this river mud
pulls me further down.
John's at my side, but he's sitting on firmer ground.

John says I look at the moon and the stars,
these days, more often than I look into his eyes.
And I can't disagree, so I don't say nothing.
I just stare on past his face at Venus rising,
like a shining speck of hope
hanging over the horizon.

With each passing year that I sit here
that horizon seems to inch just that much nearer
and all that appears on it seems as clear as spit.
But if there's one thing in my life
that these years have taught
it's that you can always see it coming,
but you can never stop it.

Speed River at my feet running low and flat,
I'm sitting here burning daylight,
thinking about the past
and that distance out there
where the earth meets the sky.
The slightest move and this river mud
pulls me further down.
John's at my side,
but he's not noticing that I'm drowning.

SOMETHING MORE BESIDES YOU

One foot stands before the crib
the other by the casket.
A question formed upon stilled lips
is passed on but never asked.

I guess I believe that there's a point
to what we do.
But I ask myself, "is there
something more besides you?"

Two are born to cross
their paths, their lives, their hearts.
If by chance one turns away
are they forever lost?

I guess I believe that there's a point
to what we do.
But I ask myself, "is there
something more besides you?"

This morning I awoke,
the bed warm where it once was cold.
Small blessings laid upon us.
Small mysteries slowly unfold.

Yet I still wonder is there a point
to what we do?
'Cause I kind of doubt
that there is something more besides you.

Although it's hard to find the point
to what we do.
Do I dare believe that there is
something more besides you?

HOLD ON TO ME

If you offered me a shade of blue
would I return it saying that it was too
dark or light?
Or would I see it for the precious thing
that it might one day be?
Hold on to me.

If you offered me a point of view
would I dismiss it saying that it was too
black and white?
Or would I see it as the special thing
that it would no doubt be?
Hold on to me.

I'll hold on to this gift we share,
it is as slippery as it is rare.
I'll hold on to that feeling
of waking and finding you there.
I'll hold on to you and you hold on to me.

If I asked you for a simple thing
would you do it without too much thinking or fuss?
Would you see it for the precious thing
that it would surely be?
Hold on to me.

Hold on to me.

GOOD FRIDAY

Sat at my window, watched the world
wake up this morning.
Purple sky slowly turning golden.
Distant elms so orange you'd swear they're burning.

All this flowing water
has got my mind wandering.
Do you ever finally reach a point of knowing?
Or do you just wake up one day and say, "I am going"?

What will I tell you
when you ask me why I'm crying?
Will I point above at the Red Tail gracefully soaring?
Or down below where its prey is quietly trembling?

Two thousand years ago Jesus is left there hanging.
Purple sky slowly turning golden.
Cowards at his feet, loudly laughing.
Loved ones stumbling homeward their worlds reeling.
Red Tail above my head quietly soaring.
Waters turn from ice, creek is roaring.
He says, "enough of all this shit I am going."

DARKLING DAYS

The beautiful is not chosen.
The chosen becomes beautiful.
The beautiful is not chosen.
The chosen becomes beautiful.

Please do not forsake me now,
sparkling gone
with darkling days.
I drift at times, I know it's true,
but I always drift on back to you.

The beautiful is not chosen.
The chosen becomes beautiful.

I have never tired of
manna falling from above:
when conscious thought
meets careless heart
and two lost souls find one fresh start.

Lie with me upon the earth,
feel its curve beneath our spines.
Soon we'll follow it around,
one lost soul
finally found.

The beautiful is not chosen.
The chosen becomes beautiful.

These are known as darkling days;
rhyming schemes gone askew,
crackling gifts of light and air,
exploding worlds,
ours to share.

The beautiful is not chosen.
The chosen becomes beautiful.

THOSE FINAL FEET

Place my body on the funeral pyre,
cut it loose to float downstream,
leave it frozen on a mountain top,
suspend it high to be picked clean.

You said never to grow old,
but you forgot to tell me how.
You said never to grow old
and then sank your teeth into those final feet.

Last night I dreamt of owls at my window.
I knew that time was winding down.
Turned to tell you of my premonition,
changed my mind and lay back down.

You said never to grow old,
but you forgot to tell me how.
You said never to grow old
and then sank your teeth into those final feet.

No sense wasting the time you got,
you've got to walk down every road.
No sense pretending that you're what you're not,
when you've got to shoulder every load.

You said never to grow old,
but you forgot to tell me how.
You said never to grow old,
and then sank your teeth into those final feet.

Cut it loose, cut it loose, cut it loose.

You said never to grow old,
but you forgot to tell me how.
You said never to grow old,
and then you sank your teeth into those final feet.

CLOSE MY EYES

I want to walk away
like Judas from the table.
Turn my back
and walk away.

I want to close my eyes
like that novice at the altar.
Bow my head
and close my eyes.

Sorrow took Love's splintered hands
and waltzed her 'cross a painted floor.
Whispered softly in her ear,
"let's get outta here."

I'm going to breathe the air
that my children will be breathing.
Breathe them out
and breathe them in again.

Turmoil took Love's dusty book,
cracked its spine in two.
Read aloud her simple lines,
cracked a wicked smile.

I want to close my eyes
like that novice at the altar.
Bow my head
and close my eyes.

Bow my head
and close my eyes.

SMALL SWIFT BIRDS

I've been told that it's just the way life goes.
Once the wildest river, is now a trickle to the sea.
The peak we risk our lives to scale becomes dirt beneath our feet.
The wisdom of a life time always disappears untapped.
Paradise once given will always be taken back.
And the love you hang your life upon will start to slowly crack.

I have seen people suffocate the dream.
Forgetting to turn that one last time while she watches through the door.
Focusing on the garbage that she use to ignore.
Thinking she looks so beautiful but not yelling it out loud.
He should have stopped to kiss her before he headed out.
Just forgetting how fucking lucky you are to have found her in such a crowd.

But we've seen a cloud of starlings rising on a crisp autumn day.
We were handed the weight of a child sleeping and bore her away.
We've tasted the tears that fall when saying goodbye forever.
And we've seen the silver from a waxing moon wash upon the shore.

I have heard about the lives of small swift birds.
They dazzle with their colour and their deftness through the air.
Just a simple glimpse will keep you simply standing there.
Legendary journeys made on fragile hollow wings.
The night skies rich with whistling each and every spring.
And then there's the day we look for them and can't find them anywhere.

I've been told that it's just the way life goes.

THOUSAND YEAR PRAYER

Here we all are at the end of "the century of beauty lost."
We greedily ate what you gave us, the rest we tossed.
We've trapped all your rivers, paved every pass,
pulled at your sky till we caused it to rip.
But you've got Jimi Hendrix so let's call it an even split.

I've met a girl who has turned my whole world upside down.
The stars I once stretched for, now litter the ground.
I am cursed by too little, or is it too much belief,
in the strength of another man's words.
But I've got a girl, thank you Lord.

Here we all are at the start of another thousand years.
All those love stories, yet to be told.
Ours is this river asleep at our feet,
blessed by this wet autumn day.
Here we all are…

SIMON KEEPER

Jesus was a carpenter he died nailed to a wooden cross.
Irony oh irony upon me it is never lost.

Gather 'round now people, I'm here to tell a tale
about a man who walks among you, a man you each know well.
My name is Simon Keeper I had a wife and three grown kids,
a job in the towers cooking the books for the shills that grease the skids.

Irony oh irony, you are a bitter fruit to eat.
Stripped of all your beauty your flesh is none too sweet.

Now I ain't the most honest man that ever worked a skim,
I was caught with my hand in the cookie jar and brother that was it.
Fifty-four and a big black mark upon my resume,
I found selling off what you don't own might earn you the time of day.

Next, it was a letter from my darling one:
"what's yours is mine, what's mine is mine,"
sealed with a hug and kiss.
One by one my children closed their lives to me.
Lesson learned on Daddy's knee,
"give no quarter to the weak."

Irony oh irony, you are the polar seed of truth,
you grow upon the open plain the faithful you uproot.

Kicked around 'bout a year, living hand to mouth,
then one day tryin' to bum a light I felt my will give out.
Sat right down on the corner, started prayin' a little too loud.
Left my troubles far behind
when I saw them emptying their pockets out.

Irony oh irony, you are a treacherous son of a bitch,
pretending not to care about the heights you'll never reach.

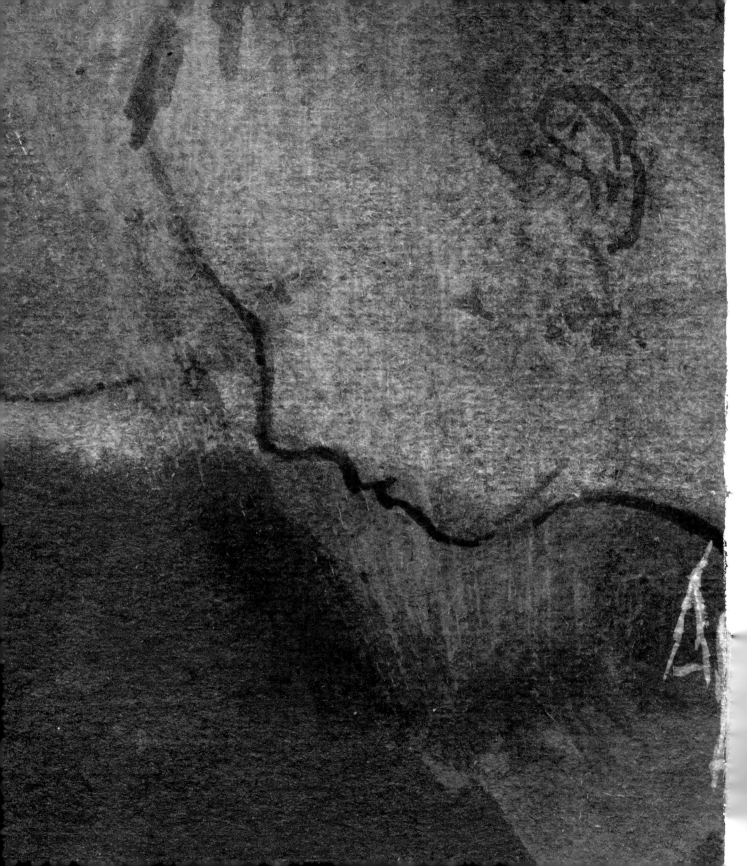

Now I won't start in preaching 'bout reaping what you sow,
this is the story of a half-hearted man,
half honest as they go.
But sit on down and rest a spell I've got another tale to tell.
About a lost young man in a far away land whose life is just too easy to sell.

Jesus was a carpenter he died nailed to a wooden cross.
Irony oh irony upon me it is never lost.

THE SLIDE

Jesus, sweet Jesus if you're listening
can you pass me to your pa.
I'm having a hard time understanding
why he's so cruel and demanding
with his love.

Darling, sweet darling keep whispering
I'll find you through this din.
Sitting and watching,
two flames busy dancing
to our love.

Grab on to this moment, inhale it
and hold it inside.
Savour its sweetness,
yearn for the slide.

Jesus, sweet Jesus if you're listening
can you pass me to your pa.
I'm having a hard time understanding
why he's so discriminating
with his love.

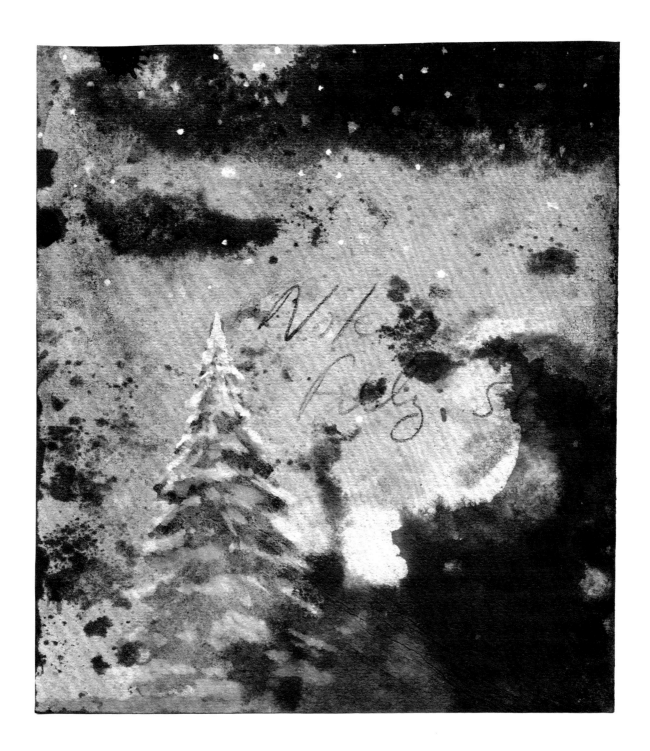

NOTES FALLING SLOW

My love swears that he is made of truth.
I do believe him though I know he lies.
I've caught him creeping 'round darkened holes.
I've caught him staring at distant skies.

I would have seen it coming, but I'm blind with age.
Too much time on the battle line.
Shut it all out just let the notes fall slow.

Slow.

My love lives inside a haze of gloom.
He fears today, what might come tomorrow.
Seeks the shadow, shuns the light.
Bleeds for knowledge, prepares for sorrow.

I would have seen it coming but I'm blind with age.
Too much time on the battle line.
Shut it all out just let the notes fall slow.

Slow.

This ain't no depression, just notes falling slow.
An early snow and notes falling slow.
Do I have the strength to bear their passion?
An early snow and notes falling slow.

COWBOY JUNKIES –
A CHRONOLOGICAL HISTORY...
OF SORTS
by Michael Timmins

1985

Michael and Peter Timmins rent and move into 547 Crawford Street in Toronto's Little Italy district and are soon joined by ("lifelong family friend") Alan Anton. The three of them attempt to soundproof the basement and turn it into a rehearsal room. Ten minutes into their first rehearsal, the neighbor of the attached house appears at their front door screaming something about a baby trying to get to sleep. The three turn their attention to the detached, cinder block garage in their backyard. Two hours into their second rehearsal, the Toronto police appear at the garage door saying something about several noise complaints. A decision is made to do some more soundproofing and, more importantly, to turn everything way down...the seed of the "Junkies Sound" is planted. John Timmins starts sitting in and a "sound" based loosely on traditional blues and post-punk rock starts to form. A vocalist is needed so Margo is asked if she is interested in sitting in. She says, "yes" but only if no one but her and Michael are present. After a few rehearsals, the others are asked to join, the instruments are turned down a little bit more and the band is complete. After a month or so in the garage, a gig is booked at The Rivoli on Toronto's Queen Street. A name for the band is needed, and, after a couple of hours of names being tossed around, Cowboy Junkies is decided upon. Like all good jam sessions, no one is quite sure where the name came from or how it was decided upon.

1986

After gigging around the Toronto area for a few months, it is decided that the time has come to record an album. In the meantime brother John has moved to Montreal and left the band. Fate intervenes when Mike and Al meet Peter Moore at a dinner party thrown by Greg Keelor of Blue Rodeo. They get to talking about recording, and Peter tells them about his passion for 2-track live recording. They all decide that this is how the Cowboy Junkies album should be recorded and a trial run is set up to take place in the band's garage/rehearsal space. The trial run and the subsequent recording, which takes place over six hours on June 28, are successful and the band's first album is born. *Whites Off Earth Now!!* is the Blues as seen through the eyes of four post-punk suburban white kids. It is self-financed and released on the band's own label, Latent Recordings.

1987

The band tours incessantly throughout Canada and the USA, picking up gigs where it can and spending a lot of time in the Southeastern USA. Traditional country music and its offspring begin to find its way onto the band's van stereo, and ideas for the next album begin to take root. On November 27 the band goes into The Church of the Holy Trinity to record their second album. Peter Moore is again in charge of the digital, 2-track live recording: the method is both primitive and state-of-the-art. Like the first album, Peter brings along just one microphone to do the recording, a Calrec ambisonic. To augment their sound, the band invites along a number of musicians: John Timmins (guitar), Jeff Bird (mandolin, harmonica, fiddle), Kim Deschamps (pedal steel, dobro, slide guitar), Jaro Czerwinec (accordion) and Steve Shearer (harmonica). The repertoire is decidedly under-rehearsed: the idea is that the arrangements and parts are to be nuanced as the day progresses. It takes seven hours to arrange the microphone and the instruments in such a way so that the band and producer are happy with the sound. The next six hours are spent working on arrangements and recording. There are no more than three or four takes recorded of each song. At the end of a very long and magical day, Peter Moore labels the tapes: Cowboy Junkies – The Trinity Session.

1988

The Trinity Session, a celebration of American song, is released on Latent Recordings and immediately begins to garner attention on the independent music scene. The band continues to tour, and major labels start to come courting. After being wined and dined by A&R reps from most North American labels ("I really like the band, but if you don't change the name you'll never get on national TV"; "I really like the band but you'll have to re-record the album"; "I really like the band but bands are like busses, wait long enough and another one comes along"; "I really like the band, but what is this Trinity Session...A demo?"), the band signs with RCA/BMG. *The Trinity Session* is re-released untouched, the band keeps its name and, later in the year, appears on "Saturday Night Live" with many more national television shows to follow. Peter Leak is signed as a manager. The band plays a showcase for BMG International in a bullring on the Gold Coast of Spain; Gene Simmons is in attendance (as a rep for Israel) and the Japanese rep, sitting directly in front of the stage, snores loudly as the band plays on.

1989

More touring (the touring band includes Jeff Bird, Jaro Czerwinec and Kim Deschamps) to many parts of the world, including Winnipeg and Tokyo, where for the first and last time in the band's history, the audience storms the stage at the end of the show. More TV appearances. More touring. Recording is begun, abandoned, restarted, refined, aborted, completed, ended and finally finished on their third album, *The Caution Horses*, a meditation on lost love. The album is recorded live off the studio floor at Eastern Studios in Toronto's Yorkville district, with the touring band and David Houghton on percussion. Peter Moore co-produces along with Michael Timmins, and Tom Henderson engineers.

1990

The Caution Horses is released. The band hooks up with legendary Texas singer-songwriter Townes Van Zandt who tours with them throughout North America. Townes teaches them how to play craps and how to spot a decent Brandy Alexander. Townes writes

"Cowboy Junkies Lament" for the band and they, in turn, write "Townes Blues."

1991

The band undertakes a Summer tour in support of Bruce Hornsby during which Margo comes down with pneumonia. All touring stops and the band takes a much-needed sabbatical. Writing is begun for *Black Eyed Man*. Grant Avenue Studios in Hamilton, Ontario is chosen as the place to record the album. Bob Doidge and John Oliviera share the engineering and advice duties. Throughout the winter the band heads to Hamilton to record a song or two at a time. A wide range of musicians are invited to participate in the sessions. The tracks are eventually mixed at Eastern Studios by Tom Henderson and Peter Moore.

1992

Black Eyed Man is released, and another world tour is launched. The album is made up of a series of vignettes centered around the theme of love and the relationships/complications it spawns. The touring band this time out includes: Jeff Bird on mandolin and harmonica, Spencer Evans on piano, organ and clarinet, and Ken Myhr on guitar. John Prine and his band share the bill for the North American leg of the tour. Margo joins John on stage each night for "Angel From Montgomery" and John joins the band each night for "If You Were The Woman And I Was the Man." The band plays Royal Albert Hall, London. They also play St Petersburg, Russia.

1993

The band gets to work at Big White on arrangements for album five. They invite Ken Myhr in on the rehearsals and then to join them at Studio 306 in downtown Toronto. *Pale Sun, Crescent Moon* is recorded (with Robert Cobban engineering) over the course of a couple of weeks and released later in the year: sun-moon, yin-yang, dark-light, hot-cold, male-female. The band once again takes to the road (this time with Jeff Bird and Ken Myhr in the touring band). It soon becomes apparent that the band and its record label have stopped "communicating." The band asks for its release from its contract and it is graciously granted.

1994

The band stops moving for the first time in five years and takes a break for the first half of the year. In the Fall the band heads off to Rock Island (a tiny island, with a tiny cottage, in the middle of a tiny lake, a couple of hours NE of Toronto) to start work on the songs that will become *Lay It Down*.

1995

A deal with Geffen Records is signed, and, in June, the band heads to Athens, Georgia to start work, with John Keane as co-producer, on *Lay It Down*, their first Geffen Records CD. *200 More Miles*, a 2-disc collection of live performances stretching over ten years, is released by BMG/RCA as part of the termination agreement.

1996

Lay It Down is released: songs about the fear of the unknown path ahead. The band hits the road again. This time Jeff Bird and Dave Henry (on cello and guitar) are in the touring band. They play Slovenia. They play Sardinia. They play Sudbury. They open a number of shows for Sting and learn a few new yoga positions.

1997

Michael takes up residence at Maidens Mill, a magical spot located two hours NNE of Toronto. Throughout the year, the band visits Maidens Mill for recreation and work. The songs for *Miles From Our Home* begin to take shape and everyone's cross-country ski skills improve immensely. Songs of frustration, blasphemy, death, anger and love. The English producer John Leckie is contacted and invited aboard. *Miles From Our Home* is recorded in downtown Toronto at McLear Place and Chemical studios. Proceedings are moved eastward to London and Abbey Road Studios for a few overdubs, some string sessions and mixing. Thousands of dollars and many pints later, most of the mixes are scrapped and the album is re-mixed in Los Angeles by Chris Lord-Algee.

1998

The album is finished and so is the record company. The first of many mergers to come in the recording industry decimates Geffen. Many phone calls are made, and none is answered. *Miles From Our Home* is released and disappears. The nadir. In the meantime, to boost their spirits, the band once again takes to the road inviting Over The Rhine to join them as an opening act and as sidemen (and women). By year's end, the band is released from its contract.

1999

The band severs a ten-year relationship with its manager, Peter Leak, and decides to venture back to its independent roots. Latent Recordings is re-animated and releases *Rarities, B-Sides and Slow, Sad Waltzes*. Cowboyjunkies.com appears on the scene. The Waltz Across America tours begin with the Summer Waltz. Karin Bergquist and Linford Detweiler remain in the touring band (Jeff Bird is also, of course, along for the ride).

2000

The Clubhouse, the band's rehearsal/recording space, is christened. It is located only a few blocks from their original space on Crawford Street. *Waltz Across America* (a live disc documenting the WAA tour) is released on Latent Recordings and is made available exclusively through cowboyjunkies.com. A deal is struck with Rounder Records in the USA, Cooking Vinyl in the UK and Universal Canada to license, distribute and market future albums. Recording for the next studio album is done between tour breaks at Chemical Studio in Toronto with the full touring band on the floor and with Daryl Smith behind the board.

2001

Open is released; songs set at life's crossroads. More touring. More touring. More touring. Simon Kendal, Vince Jones and Linford occupy the keyboard position at various points in the tour. September 11th is spent in a Tampa hotel. The band, along with the rest of the world, stares in disbelief at their TV sets. The tour continues two days later in Gainesville at one of the worst venues the band has ever played; it ranks as one of the worst gigs in the band's history. A few days later in Texas the band plays gigs in Houston and Dallas and experiences a transcendent connection